Zen Bunnies

ALSO BY BUDDHA AND THE EDITORS AT MANGO PUBLISHING

Zen Dogs

Zen Cats

Zen Kittens

Zen Puppies

Zen Bunnies

MEDITATIONS
FOR THE WISE MINDS
OF BUNNY LOVERS

Buddha
and the editors of
Mango Publishing

Cover Design: Elina Diaz
Layout & Design: Elina Diaz & Roberto Núñez

For permission requests, please contact the publisher at:
Mango Publishing Group
2850 Douglas Road, 3rd Floor
Coral Gables, FL 33134 USA
info@mango.bz

For special orders, quantity sales, course adoptions and corporate sales,
please email the publisher at sales@mango.bz. For trade and wholesale
sales, please contact Ingram Publisher Services at customer.service@
ingramcontent.com or +1.800.509.4887.

Zen Bunnies: Meditations for the Wise Minds of Bunny Lovers

ISBN: (print) 978-1-63353-798-9, (ebook) 978-1-63353-799-6
Library of Congress Control Number: 2018949978
BISAC category code: OCC010000—BODY, MIND & SPIRIT / Mindfulness
& Meditation

Printed in the United States of America

TABLE OF CONTENTS

VIRTUE   71

TRUTH   85

ETERNITY

CREDITS

MIND
AND
BODY

VERSE 1

To keep the body in good health
is a duty...otherwise we shall
not be able to keep our mind
strong and clear.
—Buddha

Health is holistic: we cannot strengthen our mind without working to strengthen our body. We cannot strengthen our body without working to strengthen our mind. That's why bunnies eat leafy greens and carrots, of course.

VERSE 2

To a mind that is still, the whole
universe surrenders.
—Chuang Tzu

When we maintain a calm mind, we find that
everything around us becomes achievable as we begin
to take things as they are.

VERSE 3

Calmness of mind does not mean you should stop your activity. Real calmness should be found in activity itself. We say, "It is easy to have calmness in inactivity, it is hard to have calmness in activity, but calmness in activity is true calmness.
—Shunryu Suzuki

Don't allow chaos to take over—instead keep a level head in the ultimate game of mind over matter to acquire the purest form of tranquility.

VERSE 4

If your mind is empty, it is always ready for anything, it is open to everything. In the beginner's mind there are many possibilities, but in the expert's mind there are few.
—Shunryu Suzuki

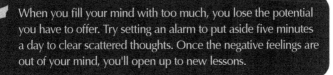

When you fill your mind with too much, you lose the potential you have to offer. Try setting an alarm to put aside five minutes a day to clear scattered thoughts. Once the negative feelings are out of your mind, you'll open up to new lessons.

VERSE 5

Not till your thoughts cease all their branching here and there, not till you abandon all thoughts of seeking for something, not till your mind is motionless as wood or stone, will you be on the right road to the Gate.
—Huang Po

Letting go of vain desires and exercising true stillness of your mind leads you on the right path beyond this life.

VERSE 6

In a mind clear as still water,
even the waves, breaking, are
reflecting it's light.
—Dogen Zenji

To an enlightened mind, difficult problems become lessons of
wisdom and mindfulness.

18

VERSE 7

When an ordinary man attains knowledge, he
is a sage; when a sage attains understanding,
he is an ordinary man.
—Zen Proverb

It is better to be an ordinary person who is capable of
understanding others than it is to be an expert who refuses to
exercise empathy.

VERSE 8

Nothing ever goes away until it has taught us
what we need to know.
—Pema Chödrön

There is no point in trying to push away hardships.
Instead, allow them to teach us.

VERSE 9

Have a mind that is open to
everything and attached to nothing.
—Tilopa

Do not hold onto old knowledge and refuse to learn
new things. Be adaptable.

VERSE 10

Sometimes you need to sit lonely on the floor in a quiet room in order to hear your own voice and not let it drown in the noise of others.
—Charlotte Eriksson

Don't give yourself to the thoughts of others. Take the time to meditate in silence. When bunnies kick back to their side and stretch out, this is the ultimate position for meditation.

VERSE 11

The fool who knows he is a
fool is that much wiser.
—Buddha

It is better to know our faults than to act as if we have none.

VERSE 12

We are shaped by our thoughts; we
become what we think.
—Buddha

Protect your mind from negativity and malice.
Fill it, instead, with calmness and truth.

VERSE 13

Be master of mind rather than mastered by mind.
—Zen Proverb

Unmastered thoughts should not control our actions.

VERSE 14

Believe nothing, no matter where you read it, or who said it, no matter if I have said it, unless it agrees with your own reason and your own common sense.
—Buddha

Do not declare anything truth without first examining it closely. Why else do bunnies sniff their food before taking a bite?

VERSE 15

Health for both mind and body comes from not mourning over the past, not worrying about the future, but to live the present moment wisely.
—Bukkyo Dendo Kyokai

We cannot control every detail of our future or go back and change our past. Worrying about either is useless. Focus on the now.

VERSE 16

All that we are is the result of what we have thought. The mind is everything. What we think we become.
—Buddha

Our thoughts become our actions. It is important to be careful of what we choose to think, as this shapes our identity.

VERSE 17

Not thinking about anything is Zen. Once you know this, walking, sitting, or lying down, everything you do is Zen.
—Bodhidharma

We do not need to do anything special to practice Zen. It is the stillness of mind as we do all things. Zen bunny stays zen all day!

VERSE 18

All wrongdoing arises because of mind. If mind is transformed can wrongdoing remain?
—Buddha

If we focus on transforming our mind, our actions will follow.

VERSE 19

It is the power of the mind to be
unconquerable.
—Seneca

When we put our mind to it, we can do anything.

VERSE 20

As a bee gathering nectar does not harm or
disturb the color & fragrance of the flower; so
do the wise move through the world.
—Buddha

We must be symbiotic creatures. Do not destroy, but
learn, use, and give back to the world.

VERSE 21

Through our eyes, the universe is perceiving itself. Through our ears, the universe is listening to its harmonies. We are the witnesses through which the universe becomes conscious of its glory, of its magnificence.
—Alan Watts

Appreciate the natural workings of the world you create. As the floppy ears of a bunny perk up to every rustle of the wind, so should you learn to take in all sensations.

VERSE 22

Those who are awake, live in a state of
constant amazement.
—Buddha

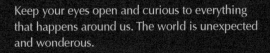

Keep your eyes open and curious to everything
that happens around us. The world is unexpected
and wonderous.

VERSE 23

The idea has come to me that what I want now to do is to saturate every atom. I mean to eliminate all waste, deadness, superfluity: to give the moment whole; whatever it includes.
—Virginia Woolf

When we do anything, we need to do it with our whole selves. Otherwise, we do not experience the moment in its fullness.

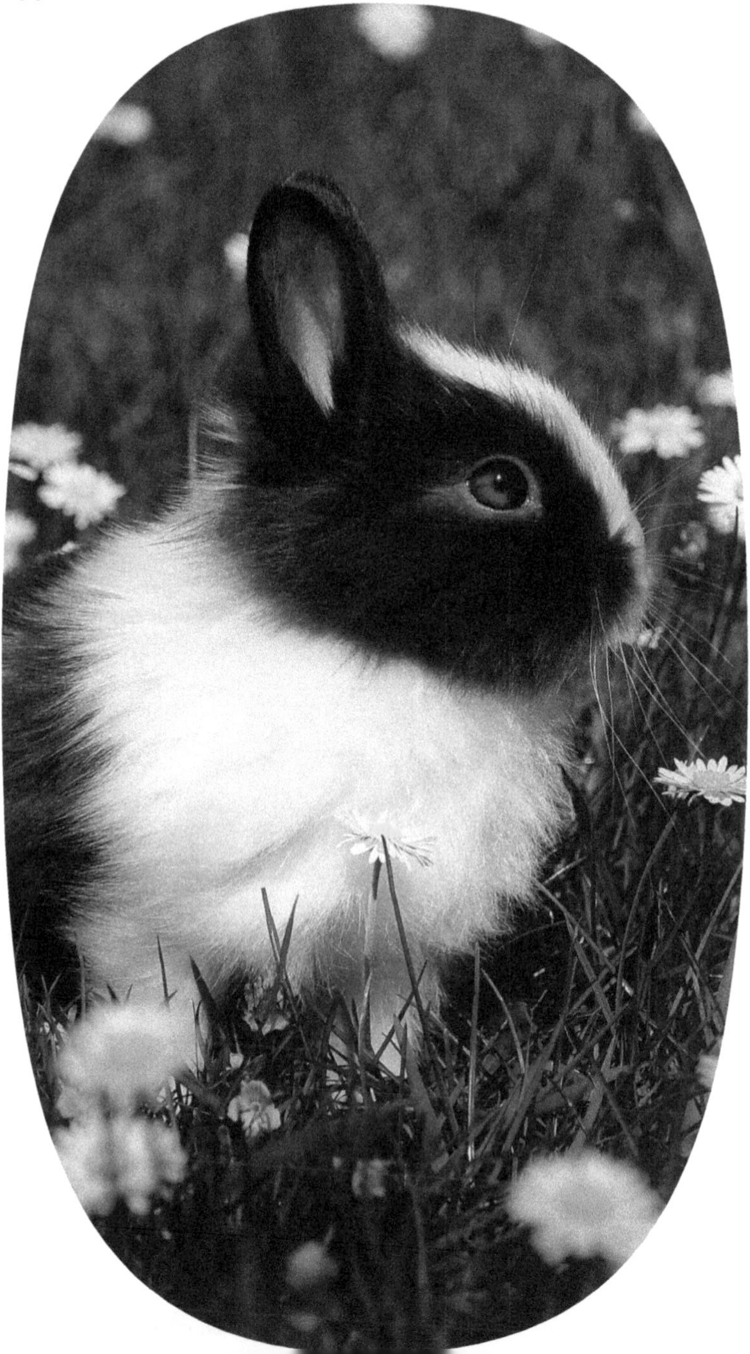

VERSE 24

Life isn't as serious as the mind
makes it out to be.
—Eckhart Tolle

Don't stress by overthinking. Bunnies don't stress because
they just eat, nap, and repeat. They've got the right idea.

HAPPINESS

VERSE 25

Step outside for a while—calm
your mind. It is better to hug
a tree than to bang your head
against a wall continually.
—Rasheed Ogunlaru

It is important to take the time to breathe in some fresh
air to let go of anger and frustration.

VERSE 26

Happiness is here, and now.
—Thích Nhất Hạnh

We do not need to go anywhere or do anything to attain happiness; we just need to acknowledge it in the moment.

VERSE 27

It is in the nature of things that joy
arises in a person free from remorse.
—Buddha

Do not wallow in regret. Learn from the past, move
forward, and be happy like a bunny in a meadow.

VERSE 28

The search for happiness is one of the chief
sources of unhappiness.
—Eric Hoffer

Time is wasted in the search for things we do not have.
Seeing what we do have and appreciating these joys is
the answer. What do you appreciate?

VERSE 29

Your vision will become clear only when you look into your heart. Who looks outside, dreams.
Who looks inside, awakens.
—Carl Jung

Happiness will not be found if we search for it outside of ourselves. Joy comes from within us

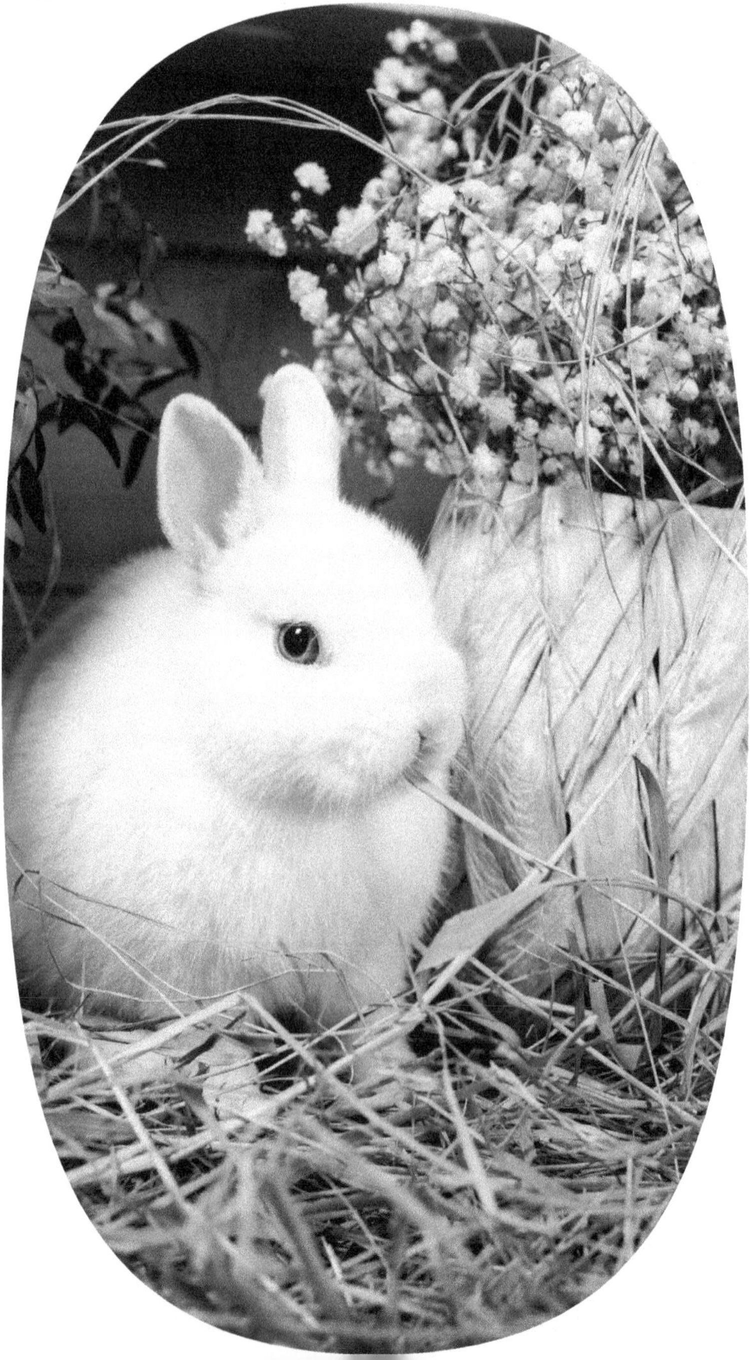

VERSE 30

The purpose of our lives is to be happy.
—Dalai Lama

Thankfulness, inner peace, and a calm mind bring us bliss.
There is no other purpose than to seek those states.

VERSE 31

There is no path to happiness:
happiness is the path.
—Buddha

When we search for happiness, we are
missing the point. Happiness is all around us,
just look right in front of you.

VERSE 32

The aim of spiritual life is to awaken a joyful freedom,
a benevolent and compassionate heart in spite of
everything.
—Jack Kornfield

Don't allow negative thoughts or experiences
to darken your temperament.

VERSE 33

Life is not about waiting for the
storms to pass...It's about learning
how to dance in the rain.
—Vivian Greene

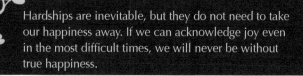

Hardships are inevitable, but they do not need to take
our happiness away. If we can acknowledge joy even
in the most difficult times, we will never be without
true happiness.

VERSE 34

Radiate boundless love towards
the entire world.
—Buddha

Love all, no matter who they are or what they do.

VERSE 35

Be kind whenever possible.
It is always possible.
—Dalai Lama

Even on our worst days, we are capable of being kind.
That kindness grows and affects everyone around us,
including ourselves and...our pets.

VERSE 36

If you want to learn, teach. If you need inspiration, inspire others. If you're sad, cheer someone up.
—Leo Babauta

How we treat others is how we treat ourselves. Benevolent acts become us. What is going to be your act of kindness today?

VERSE 37

In the end, just three things matter:
How well we have lived
How well we have loved
How well we have learned to let go
—Jack Kornfield

Earthly success is fleeting, but love and understanding
will continue to affect the world long after we leave it.

VERSE 38

Inspiring others towards happiness
brings you happiness.
—Zen Proverb

Like a bunny yawn, joy is contagious. Causing others
happiness will spread that happiness to everyone,
including ourselves.

VERSE 39

If you light a lamp for somebody,
it will also brighten your path.
—Buddha

Showing love to others brings with it a warm light
that radiates all in its cast.

VERSE 40

Thousands of candles can be
lit from a single candle, and
the life of the candle will not
be shortened. Happiness never
decreases by being shared.
—Buddha

Our happiness is not finite. The more we share it, the more there is.

VERSE 41

Happiness will never come to those who fail to
appreciate what they already have.
—Buddha

Happiness and thankfulness go hand in hand. If we
are always longing for what we do not have, we will
never find room in our hearts for joy.

VERSE 42

Do not let the behavior of others destroy your
inner peace.
—Dalai Lama

We cannot control others, but we can control how
we allow them to affect us.

VERSE 43

When I feel like dancing, I dance. I don't care
if anyone else is dancing or if everyone else is
laughing at me. I dance.
—Rachel Danson

Regardless of what others are doing around us,
we should do what brings us joy. For all we know,
we may bring them joy, too.

VERSE 44

If the problem has a solution, worrying is pointless; in the end the problem will be solved. If the problem has no solution, there is no reason to worry, because it can't be solved.
—Zen Proverb

All in all, do not worry.
Things work themselves out and move on.

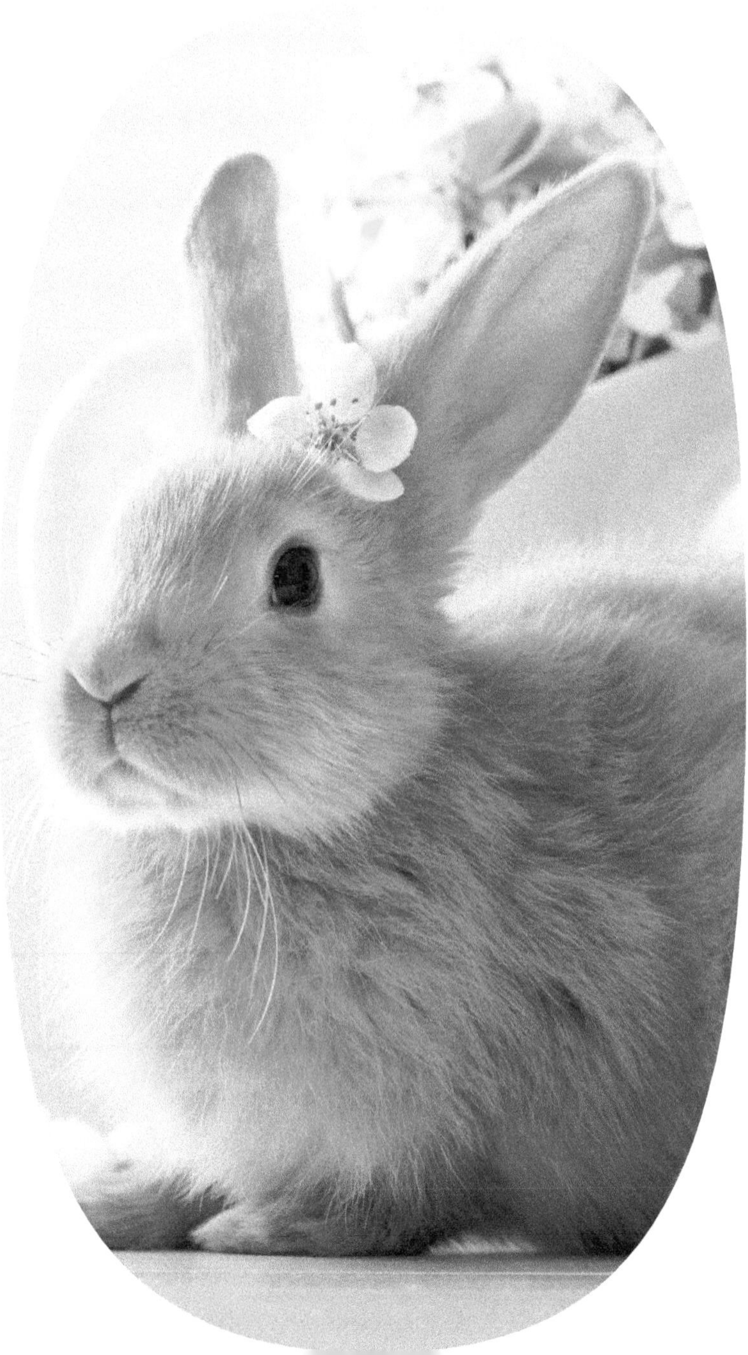

VERSE 45

Almost everything that I've
ever worried about has never
happened
—Ian Tucker

Worry fills our hearts and minds with what could be, but is not.
There is no point in lending it our attention.

VERSE 46

The world is like a mirror you see. Smile and
your friend will smile back.
—Japanese Zen Proverb

Those around us will reflect our own actions and
choices. If we choose to be happy, others will follow.

VERSE 47

Happiness is your nature. It is not wrong to desire it. What is wrong is seeking it outside when it is inside.
—Ramana Maharshi

What is outside of us can never become a part of us. Material possessions, earthly success, another's acceptance—they do not control our happiness. Our happiness comes from within.

VIRTUE

VERSE 48

To enjoy good health, to bring
true happiness to one's family,
to bring peace to all, one must
first discipline and control one's
own mind. If a man can control
his mind he can find the way to
Enlightenment, and all wisdom and
virtue will naturally come to him.
—Buddha

Learn and constantly be aware of that learning.
Once we understand how we think, like a ripple,
it will affect everything around us.

VERSE 49

Full of love for all things in the world,
practicing virtue, in order to benefit
others, this man alone is happy.
—Buddha

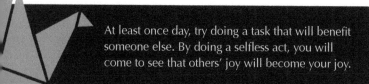

At least once day, try doing a task that will benefit
someone else. By doing a selfless act, you will
come to see that others' joy will become your joy.

VERSE 50

If a man's mind becomes pure, his surroundings
will also become pure.
—Buddha

A pure mind attracts a pure environment,
whether that be social positivity or a fresh
perspective of the world.

VERSE 51

Just as treasures are uncovered from the earth, so virtue appears from good deeds, and wisdoms from a pure and peaceful mind. To walk safely through the maze of human life, one needs the light of wisdom and the guidance of virtue.
—Buddha

Our worth is defined by inspiring interactions and an open mind willing to grow.

VERSE 52

May I be a light for those in need of light.
May I be a bed for those in need of rest.
May I be a servant for those in need of service,
for all embodied beings.
—Shantideva

Being caring and generous influences the way you
are treated, and moreover, how the person you
treat will treat others.

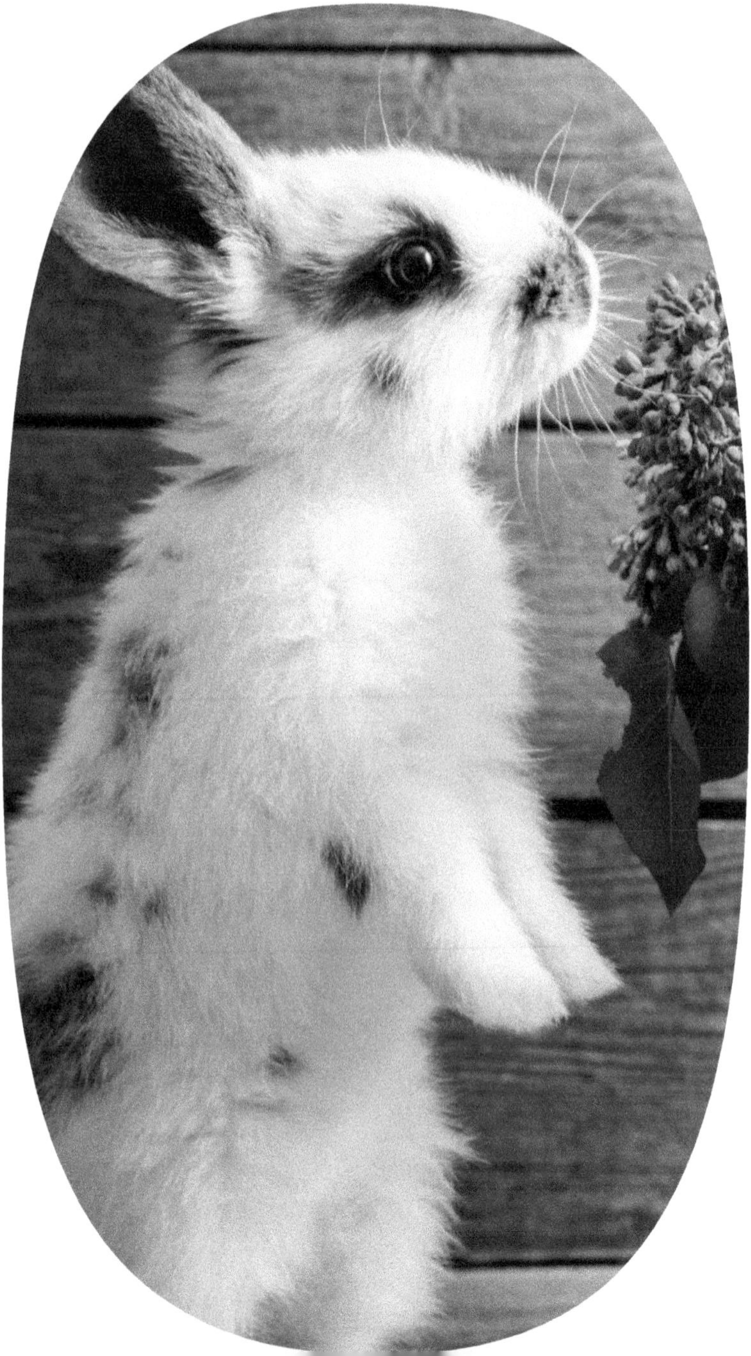

VERSE 53

The fragrance of sandalwood
and rosebay does not travel far.
But the fragrance of virtue rises
to the heavens.
—Buddha

Temporal impressions don't last, but the actions of a good
deed is something people remember for a lifetime.

VERSE 54

Follow the way of virtue. Follow the way joyfully through this world and on beyond. —Buddha

Follow the virtuous path like a zen bunny by practicing a good deed every day. It doesn't have to be a big one—it can be as small as opening the door for someone. Or sharing your hay.

VERSE 55

The glorious chariots of kings wear out, and the body wears out and grows old; but the virtue of the good never grows old.
—Buddha

Remember that nobody remembers what you wore today (or how good your fur looks), but only how you treated them.

VERSE 56

The virtue of the candle lies not in the wax that
leaves its trace, but in its light.
—Antoine De Saint-Exupéry

It's not about the messy parts that take a lot out of you,
but in how your effort creates a lasting light of wisdom.

VERSE 57

Nothing is more disobedient than an undisciplined mind. Nothing is more obedient than a disciplined mind.
—Buddha

To find virtue is not as easy task. You must start by fixing yourself, not other people. Train yourself to exercise control and your mind will follow with deftness.

TRUTH

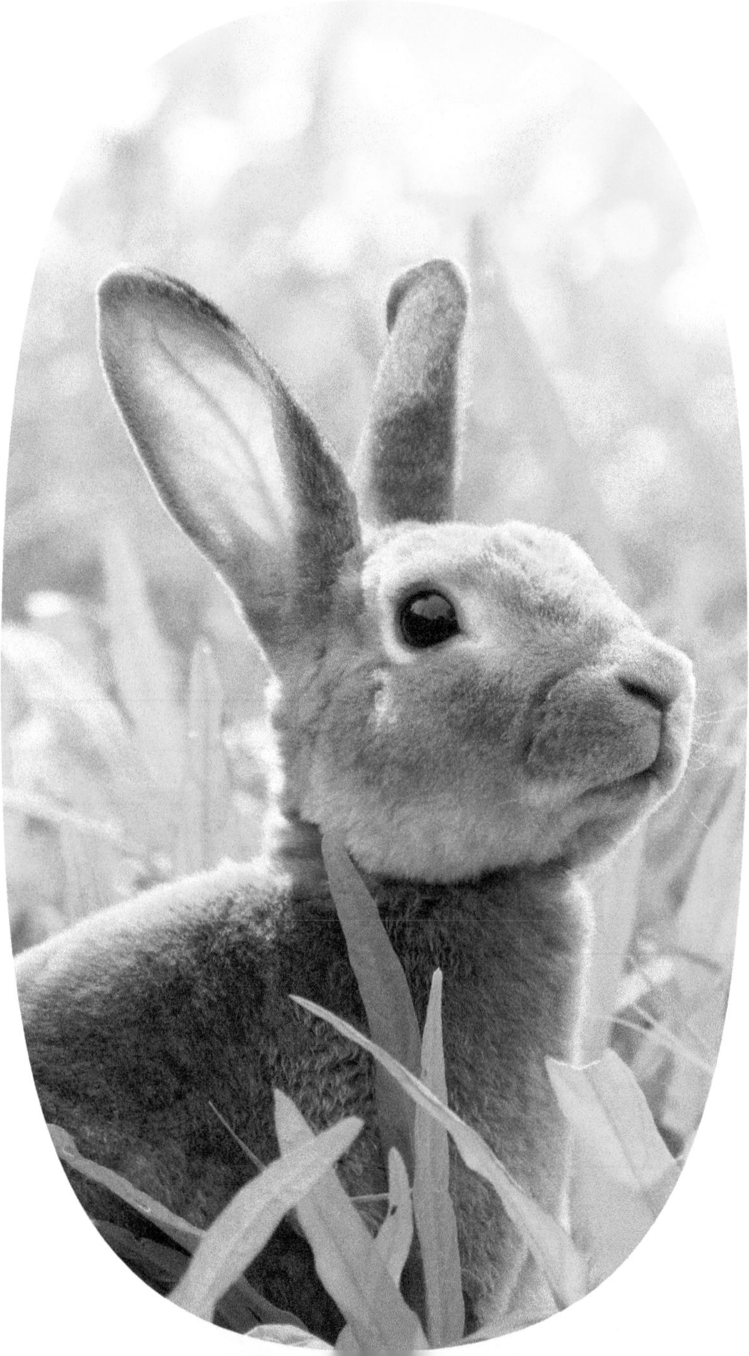

VERSE 58

The secret of Zen is just two
words: not always so.
—Shunryu Suzuki Roshi

That doesn't sound the way it is supposed to, right? Or does it...?
It might make you uncomfortable, but the foremost philosophy of
Buddhism is detachment. Embrace the uncomfortable and accept
that you are not always in control.

VERSE 59

It is only with the heart that one can see rightly;
what is essential is invisible to the eye.
—Antoine De Saint-Exupéry

We are often distracted from what is truly important in life.
What do you think is "essential" to you? Like your fluffy
pet, start thinking with your heart today.

VERSE 60

Meditation practice is often regarded as a good and in fact excellent way to overcome warfare in the world: our own warfare as well as greater warfare.
—Chögyam Trungpa Rinpoche

Breathe, reflect, and consider your place and purpose in times of discord. You will be better able to embrace the events around you from a mind state of peace rather than stress.

VERSE 61

Peace between counties must rest on the solid
foundation of love between individuals.
—Mahatma Gandhi

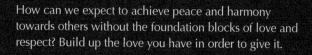

How can we expect to achieve peace and harmony
towards others without the foundation blocks of love and
respect? Build up the love you have in order to give it.

VERSE 62

In joy and sorrow all are equal, thus be guardian of all, as of yourself.
—Shantideva

Suffering and happiness is the human condition. Accept the pain of others and of ourselves to be free.

VERSE 63

In the garden of gentle sanity
may you be bombarded by
coconuts of wakefulness.
—Chögyam Trungpa Rinpoche

Complacency is simple to achieve, but very stagnant.
Crack your head open (not literally) to challenge yourself—seek
and invite new wisdom and truth.

VERSE 64

Three things cannot be long hidden: the sun, the
moon, and the truth.
—Buddha

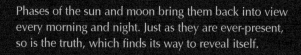

Phases of the sun and moon bring them back into view
every morning and night. Just as they are ever-present,
so is the truth, which finds its way to reveal itself.

VERSE 65

A man is not called wise because he talks and talks again; but if he is peaceful, loving and fearless then he is in truth called wise.
—Gautama Buddha

One cannot be wise just by their words. One is called wise through their honest actions.

VERSE 66

Peace comes from within.
Do not seek it without.
—Buddha

Bunnies can be on their own, don't depend
your inner peace on external forces.

VERSE 67

We are shaped by our thoughts; we become what we think. When the mind is pure, joy follows like a shadow that never leaves.
—Buddha

Become what you believe.
Rid your mind of hate and happiness will follow.

VERSE 68

To believe in something, and
not to live it, is dishonest.
—Mahatma Gandhi

Do what you advise others to do. If you go against what you
say or think, then you're false to those dogmas.

VERSE 69

Truth never damages a cause that is just.
—Mahatma Gandhi

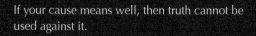

If your cause means well, then truth cannot be
used against it.

VERSE 70

Stop, stop. Do not even speak.
The ultimate truth is not even to think.
—Buddha

Truth is not in empty words or copious thoughts.
Quiet bunnies know the ultimate truth
from all that they observe.

VERSE 71

Even if you are a minority of one,
the truth is the truth.
—Mahatma Gandhi

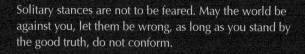

Solitary stances are not to be feared. May the world be
against you, let them be wrong, as long as you stand by
the good truth, do not conform.

VERSE 72

We should not attach to some fancy ideas or to some beautiful things. We should not seek for something good. The truth is always near at hand, within your reach.
—Shunryu Suzuki Roshi

Bunnies don't care if they have the fanciest hutch or bushiest tail. It's not about short-term satisfaction, but quality purpose for the soul.

VERSE 73

The true purpose of Zen is to see
things as they are, to observe things
as they are, and to let everything go
as it goes. Zen practice is to open up
our small mind.
-Shunryu Suzuki

Sometimes too much effort can be a bad thing.
Don't force change. Let things be as they were meant to be.

VERSE 74

The tongue, like a sharp knife...
Kills without drawing blood.
—Buddha

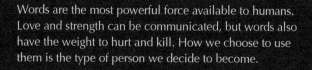

Words are the most powerful force available to humans. Love and strength can be communicated, but words also have the weight to hurt and kill. How we choose to use them is the type of person we decide to become.

VERSE 75

Morality is the basis of things and truth is the substance of all morality.
—Mahatma Gandhi

Right and wrong judgments command our moral compass. Knowing our morals to make decisions is the foundation for all truth.

VERSE 76

Honest disagreement is often a
good sign of progress.
—Mahatma Gandhi

It can be hard to see someone else's viewpoint, but when two
people can come to respect and understand their opposing
views, they are able to comprise and move forward.

VERSE 77

In the end, only three things matter: how much
you loved, how gently you lived, and gracefully
you let go of things not meant for you.
—Buddha

Letting go may be difficult, but we cannot move mountains
and force things to be. What's meant for you will come.

VERSE 78

There are only two mistakes one can make along the road to truth: not going all the way and not starting.
—Buddha

To many, starting the journey is the hardest task. To others, it is finishing it. Meditate upon what is the most difficult for you and how you can overcome this mental challenge.

VERSE 79

What is truth? A difficult question; but I have solved it for myself by saying that it is what the "Voice within" tells you.
—Buddha

Brief moments should be taken to drown out outside noise and listen to your conscience, if you will.

ETERNITY

VERSE 80

Hatred never ceases by hatred,
but by love alone is healed. This
is an ancient and eternal law.
—Dhammapada, Verse 5

Hatred will persist if you cannot move on with a loving
heart. Hang out with your bunny to remember the natural
love given and received.

VERSE 81

Train yourself to have a kind heart
always and in all situations.
—Patrul Rinpoche

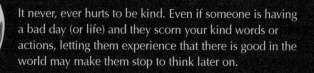

It never, ever hurts to be kind. Even if someone is having
a bad day (or life) and they scorn your kind words or
actions, letting them experience that there is good in the
world may make them stop to think later on.

VERSE 82

The everyday practice is simply to develop
a complete acceptance and openness to all
situations and emotions, and to all people,
experiencing everything totally without mental
reservations and blockages, so that one never
withdraws or centralizes into oneself.
—Dilgo Khyentse Rinpoche

Today, whatever happens, test yourself by not
responding with judgment and preconceived opinions.
Unbiased zen bunnies are open to understanding all.

VERSE 83

So you should view this fleeting world
As a star at dawn, a bubble in a stream,
A flash of lightning in a summer cloud,
A flickering lamp, a phantom, and a dream.
—Diamond Sūtra

Seize the time you have now to do what matters most.
It can be gone in an instant.

VERSE 84

Live as if you were to die tomorrow.
Learn as if you were to live forever.
—Mahatma Gandhi

Take-in and be present because every moment
we learn from will make us.

VERSE 85

Your purpose in life is to find
your purpose and give your
whole heart and soul to it.
—Buddha

Sometimes we have to get lost to find our purpose.
But once we find it, we must give everything we have
because it is the only thing to live for.

VERSE 86

I am prepared to die, but there is no cause for
which I am prepared to kill.
—Buddha

Accept that we will move on from this life,
but no one has the right to take that life from another.

VERSE 87

On the long journey of human life...
faith is the best of companions.
—Buddha

It is always good to believe in something.
Bunnies are the best of companions, too.

VERSE 88

All human unhappiness comes from not facing
reality squarely, exactly as it is.
—Buddha

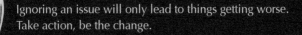

Ignoring an issue will only lead to things getting worse.
Take action, be the change.

VERSE 89

If we could see the miracle of a single flower
clearly, our whole life would change.
—Gautama Buddha

Simple wonders give us the humble
perspective we need to appreciate life.
Such as the simple wonder of our adorable pets.

VERSE 90

The universe itself is change and life itself isn't what you deem it.
—Buddha

There are things constantly changing and you must be willing to evolve in order to overcome unplanned obstacles.

VERSE 91

One moment can change a day, one day can change
a life and one life can change the world.
—Buddha

Never underestimate how powerful you can be.

VERSE 92

As a lotus flower is born in water, grows in water and rises out of water to stand above it unsoiled, so I, born in the world, raised in the world having overcome the world, live unsoiled by the world.
—Buddha

Obstacles cannot soil you, like the paws of a bunny hopping through a garden. Let them help you grow the more wiser.

VERSE 93

Be where you are; otherwise
you will miss your life.
—Buddha

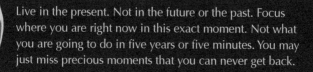

Live in the present. Not in the future or the past. Focus where you are right now in this exact moment. Not what you are going to do in five years or five minutes. You may just miss precious moments that you can never get back.

VERSE 94

Our life is shaped by our mind,
for we become what we think.
—Buddha

How we think is how we act, and therefore how we
make our decisions that define our journey.

VERSE 95

Many do not realize that we here must die. For those who realize this, quarrels end.
—The Dhammapada

Small disagreements, hate, grudges are all nothing once you realize that none of it will ever matter. We all die, we are the same in this, therefore we must treat every moment with great importance.

VERSE 96

But the scent of the good is blown against the
wind: A good man perfumes all directions.
—The Dhammapada

Like a beautiful aroma, a positive aura can be
sensed and diffused for all to take in.

CREDITS

All Photos from Shutterstock

Cover: Grigorita Ko

p. 10: Richard Peterson
p. 12: Nataliia Melnychuk
p. 13: Djem
p. 14: Dora Zett
p. 15: Dora Zett
p. 16: Dora Zett
p. 18: Dora Zett
p. 19: Melinda Nagy
p. 20: Madelein Wolfaardt
p. 21: Logra
p. 22: Trum Ronnarong
p. 24: Logra
p. 25: Momemoment
p. 26: Denise Barker
p. 27: Kaewmanee jiangsihui
p. 28: Roma Likhvan
p. 30: Fotograf Lina Johansson
p. 31: natthawatt wongkhamchan
p. 32: Bezus Iryna
p. 33: natthawatt wongkhamchan
p. 34: Skeronov
p. 36: Skeronov
p. 37: Chelmicky
p. 38: Koretnyk Anastasiia
p. 42: Annette Shaff
p. 44: Augustas Cetkauskas
p. 45: Nando Castoldi
P. 46 UNIKYLUCKK
p. 47 Logra
p. 48: Skeronov
p. 50: Leena Robinson
p. 51: Dagmar Hijmans

p. 52: Subbotina Anna
p. 53: Claudia Paulussen
p. 54: Svend77
p. 56: Dominik Belica
p. 57: Volodymyr Burdiak
p. 58: Grigorita Ko
p. 59: Richard Peterson
p. 60: Grigorita Ko
p. 62: Nadezhda V. Kulagina
p. 63: Grigorita Ko
p. 64: Logra
p. 65: Grigorita Ko
p. 66: Maya Kruchankova
p. 68: Grigorita Ko
p. 69: Smit
p. 72: Preediwat
p. 74: bmf-foto.de
p. 75: Pentium5
p. 76: Feomarty Olga
p. 77: Africa Studio
p. 78: Maya Kruchankova
p. 80: id-art
p. 81: Angel Oak Photography
p. 82: MestoSveta
p. 83: Sebastian Duda
p. 86: Mr. Joe
p. 88:Tolola
p. 89: KanphotoSS
p. 90: IM_VISUALS
p. 91: riggleton
p. 92: Maya Kruchankova
p. 94: Taa photo
p. 95: Coryn
p. 96: Eva Foreman

The Zen of Dogs and Cats

ISBN 978-1633530485
PRICE US$12.70
TRIM 5X8

ISBN 978-1633535237
PRICE US$11.52
TRIM 5X8

ISBN 978-1633535213
PRICE US$11.52
TRIM 5X8

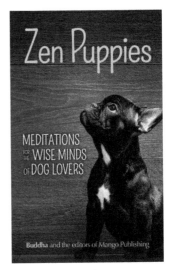

ISBN 978-1633537187
PRICE US$11.52
TRIM 5X8